Kosher International Cookbook

by
Sheilah Kaufman

WRC Publishing

Cover Design & Illustrations by Jim Haynes

Library of Congress #83-060023

ISBN 0-942320-06-9

Published by:
WRC PUBLISHING
2915 Fenimore Road
Silver Spring, Maryland 20902

This book is dedicated to those families
and individuals who maintain a Kosher
Household.

*and to Sheila Kane
who preserves the
tradition of family at
Passover.*

Love Fran 1986

TABLE OF CONTENTS

Appetizers

Salmon Mousse

Even people who don't like salmon will adore this. Also makes a great sandwich spread.

1	*medium onion cut into quarters*
½	*cup boiling water*
1 ½	*envelopes unflavored gelatin*
2	*tablespoons lemon juice*
½	*cup mayonnaise*
¼	*teaspoon paprika*
½	*teaspoon dried dill weed*
1	*small can red salmon - drained*
1	*1 pound can red salmon - drained*
1	*cup table cream*

Drain the salmon well and pick out any bits of bone.

In a blender, for about 1 minute, blend the onion, water, gelatin and lemon juice.

When well blended, add the following (in about 3 equal parts) and blend well after each addition: the mayonnaise, paprika, dill weed and both cans of salmon. When all the parts are well blended, add the cream, ⅓ cup at a time.

Grease (oil) a 6 cup mold very well (a fish shaped mold is the most appropriate).

Pour in the mousse and chill in the refrigerator for at least 3 days before serving.

One hour before serving, unmold. Do not unmold by dipping mold in hot water. Instead go around the edges with a knife, if it does not unmold then, put the mold in ½ " of hot water for 10 seconds.

If you wish, you can use olives for the eyes, scales, etc. and pimento too.

Serve with miniature rye and/or pumpernickel breads, or with crackers.

Mushroom Wine Soup

The longer it sits in the refrigerator, the better it gets.

> 2 *quarts canned beef broth or beef bouillon*
> ¾ *cup chopped onions*
> 1 *pound fresh mushrooms, sliced*
> ½ *cup chopped celery*
> 1 *clove garlic, minced*
> 2 *bay leaves*
>   *fresh ground pepper*
> 2 *tablespoons dried parsley*
> ¾ *teaspoon MSG - optional*
> 1 *teaspoon Worcestershire sauce*
> 3 *tablespoons cornstarch dissolved in ½ cup cold water*
> ¾ *cup sauterne or white wine*
> ⅓ *cup parve margarine*

In a large (4 quart or more) pot, melt margarine and saute onions, mushrooms, celery, bay leaves and parsley for about 10 minutes.

Add beef broth, pepper, MSG, Worcestershire sauce and simmer partially covered for about 1 hour.

Add cornstarch mixture and stir constantly and cook about 3 more minutes.

Remove from heat and strain. Discard everything but the sliced mushrooms.

Add mushrooms and wine to the soup and adjust seasoning to taste.

Oven Baked Stuffed Mushrooms

24 *large whole mushrooms*
2 *cloves garlic, finely-minced*
1 *stick butter*
1 *cup plain bread crumbs*
½ *cup grated cheese*
salt
fresh ground black pepper
2 *tablespoons chopped parsley*

Preheat oven to 350° F.

Remove stems from mushroom caps and chop them very fine. Saute chopped stems, along with garlic, in half of the butter.

Add the bread crumbs, cheese, salt, pepper and parsley.Remove from heat after stirring well.

In another skillet, melt 3 tablespoons of the remaining butter and saute the caps briefly.

Fill the caps with the stuffing, and place them in a shallow, well greased casserole, or baking pan.

Melt the remaining tablespoon of butter and drizzle over the tops.

Bake until very hot, about 15 minutes.

To serve as a garnish or vegetables for meats, roasts, chicken, etc. leave out the cheese and add some spices to the bread crumbs; also you can add a small amount of sauteed ground meat to the filling.

Mushroom Croustades

You can make the croustades and freeze them empty, and use them as you need them, or you can make and freeze the complete recipe.

Croustades:

24	*slices of fresh, thin-sliced white bread, with crusts removed*
2	*tablespoons soft butter*

Filling:

4	*tablespoons butter*
3	*tablespoons finely chopped shallots*
½	*pound mushrooms, fresh and finely chopped*
2	*tablespoons flour*
1	*cup whipping cream*
	pinch of salt
	dash of pepper
	pinch of cayenne
1	*tablespoon finely chopped fresh parsley*
1 ½	*tablespoons finely chopped chives*
½	*teaspoon lemon juice*
2	*tablespoons grated Swiss cheese*

Preheat oven to 400° F. Coat the insides of 24 small muffin tins (or 12 large) with the 2 tablespoons soft butter.

Cut 3″ rounds from the bread and place them carefully into the tins, molding the bread to the tin to form a little cup.

Bake the croustades for about 8-10 minutes, or until lightly brown on rims and outsides. Remove from tins, and cool. (Or freeze for future use).

Chop shallots and mushrooms very fine. In a large skillet slowly melt 4 tablespoons butter, and add shallots. Stir and cook about 3-4 minutes, then stir in mushrooms.

Mix well into butter. Stir occasionally, and cook about 15 minutes or until moisture has evaporated.

Remove skillet from heat and stir in flour. Make sure the flour is well stirred in — use a whisk if you have one.

Pour cream over mixture, return to heat, and bring to the boil, stirring constantly. As it thickens, turn heat down to simmer, and cook a minute or two to remove taste of flour.

Remove pan from heat and add seasonings. Stir well. Place mixture in a bowl to cool.

Fill croustades and sprinkle each with a few grains of cheese. Dot with a speck of butter and place on a cookie sheet. Heat for 10 minutes in the oven, and very briefly under the boiler.

These can also be used as a vegetable with fish dishes, or by eliminating the cheese, using Parve margarine, and coffee rich instead of cream, this makes a nice vegetable for roasts, chicken, etc.

Israeli

Cold Cherry Soup

This is so sweet, you could use it for a dessert.

3 *cups cold water*
1 *cup sugar*
½ *teaspoon cinnamon*
4 *cups canned sour (tart) cherries, pitted and drained*
1 *tablespoon cornstarch*
¼ *cup whipping cream (or coffee rich if this is to be used with meats, etc.)*
¾ *cup dry red wine, chilled*

In a large pot, combine the water, sugar and cinnamon. Bring to a boil and add the cherries.

Partially cover the pan and simmer over low heat, for about 10 minutes.

Combine the cornstarch with 2 tablespoons cold water and stir into the soup.

Stirring constantly, bring the soup almost to a boil.

Reduce the heat and simmer about 2 minutes or until it is clear and slightly thickened.

Pour soup into a shallow bowl (to chill faster) and place in the refrigerator until chilled.

Before serving, chill the bowls you will serve the soup in, and stir in the cream and the wine.

Marinated Mushrooms

Can be made days ahead.

1½-2   *pounds fresh whole mushrooms*
       juice of ½ a lemon
       pinch of salt
1 ¼   *cups tarragon wine vinegar (can be made by*
       placing a crushed tablespoon of tarragon in
       wine vinegar or it can be bought ready made)
⅔   *cup olive oil*
4   *crushed garlic cloves*
1   *teaspoon thyme*
3   *sprigs parsley*
1   *bay leaf*
6   *peppercorns*
12   *coriander seeds*

Wipe off mushrooms with a damp towel, cap side up. Place mushrooms in a pan and cover with cold water to cover, add lemon juice and salt.

Bring gently to a boil; lower heat and simmer about 10 minutes. Mushrooms are now blanched.

Place mushrooms in a shallow *earthenware* dish or bowl. This avoids an acidic reaction between vinegar and metal which causes a metallic taste.

Combine the vinegar, oil, garlic and seasonings in an enamel or glass pan and bring to the boil.

Lower the heat and simmer 20 minutes.

Pour over mushrooms, and marinate them overnight in the refrigerator or for 24 hours.

Hot Cheese Puffs

A tasty tidbit that uses up any extra egg whites you might have in your freezer.

> 3   *cups sharp cheddar cheese, grated*
> ¼   *cup unsifted all purpose flour*
> ½   *teaspoon salt*
>   *dash of pepper*
> 5   *egg whites, at room temperature*
> ½   *cup unseasoned bread crumbs*
>   *salad oil or shortening for deep-frying*

Combine cheese, flour, salt and pepper; mix thoroughly.

In a large bowl, beat egg whites until stiff peaks form when beaters are slowly raised.

Gently fold in cheese mixture just until well combined with egg whites.

Shape into balls, using level tablespoon for each. Roll in bread crumbs on wax paper.

If not serving right away, place in single layer on cookie sheet, cover, and refrigerate (or freeze for longer periods).

Just before serving, heat salad oil or shortening (about 1½ " deep) in heavy skillet or electric frying pan (375⁰ F).

Deep-fry cheese balls until golden, about ½ minute. Remove with slotted spoon, and drain on paper towels. Serve hot.

Puffs will be crisp on outside with cheese melted on the inside — heavenly.

Makes about 3 dozen puffs.

Iced Tomato Soup With Dill

A delight on a hot evening, this does not have a strong tomato soup taste. It is rich and good.

6   *ripe tomatoes coarsely chopped*
1   *onion, chopped*
¼   *cup water*
    fresh ground pepper
    salt
2   *tablespoons tomato paste*
2   *tablespoons flour*
2   *cups hot chicken stock or broth*
1   *cup whipping cream (if this is to be used with meats, etc. substitute Coffee Rich®)*
    chopped dill or dill weed

Place tomatoes in a pan with onion, water, salt and pepper. Bring the water to a boil and cook briskly for about 6 or 7 minutes.

Stir in the tomato paste and mix well.

Mix the flour with a little bit of cold water to form a paste and stir this in. Blend well.

Add the chicken stock (hot) and continue to stir until the soup comes to a boil.

Remove soup from heat and press the soup through a fine sieve, using a wooden spoon to force as much of the vegetable pulp through as possible.

Stir the soup for a few minutes and then let it cool.

When soup has cooled for a little while, stir in cream and taste soup to see if it needs more salt or pepper.

Serve soup cold in glasses or bowls and sprinkle each portion with the dill before serving.

This may be made a few days ahead.

Mock Boursin

8   *ounces cream cheese, softened*
½   *teaspoon garlic powder*
1   *tablespoon finely minced fresh parsley*
½   *teaspoon finely minced chives*
½   *teaspoon dried thyme leaves, crushed*
      Pinch of dried marjoram, finely crumbled
      White pepper to taste

Using an electric mixer or a food processor, combine all the ingredients until the mixture is very smooth.

Place the cheese in a covered crock or bowl.

Refrigerate for at least 12 hours so that the flavor can develop.

To serve, spread on unflavored crackers or sliced French bread.

Serves 12.

Entrees

Beef Bourguignon

A classic French beef stew that is perfect for fall and winter entertaining. It can and should be made several days in advance because the flavor improves with age. Freezes beautifully. Serve with potatoes or noodles, French bread, and a salad.

3 *pounds beef cut into 1" cubes*
½ *cup flour seasoned with salt and pepper*
4 *tablespoons salad oil*
2 *tablespoons brandy or cognac*
1 *pound peeled whole small white onions or*
2 cans white onions, well drained
¾ *pound whole fresh mushrooms*
1 *cup red wine*
2 *beef bouillon cubes*
1 *bay leaf*
salt and pepper

Preheat oven to 300º F.

Drain beef on paper towels, and dredge in flour.

In a large heavy pot, heat oil, and when oil is hot, brown the meat over a high heat, adding more oil as needed. Remove meat as it browns. When all beef has been browned, return it to the pot.

Heat brandy in a small saucepan and ignite it with a match. Pour, flaming, over meat and when flame dies out, remove beef and set aside.

Heat a little more oil in the pot and add onions and mushrooms. Cook, stirring occasionally, until onions and mushrooms are brown.

Place beef, onions and mushrooms in a 4 quart pot or casserole that is oven-proof, unless pot you have been using is oven-proof.

Add wine, beef bouillon cubes, bay leaf, salt and pepper to taste.

Place in oven and cook, covered, 2-3 hours, or until meat is tender.

If sauce gets too thick, add a little more wine. If too thin, reduce by removing cover for last hour of cooking. In either case, check casserole about every half hour.

To prepare in advance: follow all steps, but if frozen remove from freezer morning of party. If just refrigerated, remove from refrigerator at least 3 hours before serving so it can come to room temperature. Gently reheat in slow oven 45 minutes to 1 hour. Remove bay leaf before serving.

Beef and Eggplant Provencale

This dish has many of the virtues of Boeuf Bourguignon: it can be made in advance, it is relatively inexpensive for a large crowd, and it is a perfect cold-weather company dish. However, the addition of eggplant, and the subtle flavoring of the tomato-based sauce make this dish somewhat more unique.

Beef in Wine:

⅓	*cup salad oil*
4½	*pounds beef cut in 1" cubes*
2	*pounds small white onions*
⅓	*cup flour; 1 teaspoon sugar*
2	*tablespoons flour*
	salt
½	*teaspoon dried basil leaves*
½	*teaspoon dried thyme leaves*
	fresh ground pepper
	dash ground cloves
1	*1 pound 12 ounce can tomatoes, undrained*
1½	*cups red wine*

Eggplant:

2	*medium eggplants*
3	*eggs*
1	*cup fresh bread crumbs*
¾	*cup salad oil*

Garnish:

3	*medium tomatoes*
	salt
½	*teaspoon dried thyme*
2	*tablespoons chopped parsley*

In the morning, or the night before, make Beef in Wine. In a 6 quart heavy pot, heat about 2 tablespoons of the oil.

Add beef cubes, about ⅓ at a time, and cook over high heat until well browned on all sides. Remove beef as it browns and set aside. Add more oil as needed.

Meanwhile, in a 3 quart saucepan, bring 2 quarts water to boiling and place onions in boiling water for about 3 minutes. (This will facilitate peeling them).

When onions are cool enough to handle, peel them, and add to kettle in which beef was browned. Cook until lightly browned. Remove and set aside.

Remove large pot from heat.

Stir in flour, sugar, salt, basil, thyme, pepper and cloves until well blended.

Gradually stir in tomatoes and wine.

Add bay leaves and browned beef. Bring to boiling, stirring occasionally.

Reduce heat, and simmer covered, 2½ hours. Stir occasionally, and taste sauce to make sure it is seasoned to your taste. (You may want to add more herbs and/or more sugar).

Add browned onions and cook, 40 minutes longer, or until beef and onions are tender.

Remove bay leaves. Let beef in wine cool to room temperature, and then refrigerate, covered.

A couple of hours before serving, remove beef in wine from refrigerator and let it stand at room temperature.

Meanwhile, prepare eggplant: wash eggplants, and cut crosswise into ½ " slices.

In a shallow dish, beat eggs with ¼ cup water.

Dip eggplant slices first into egg mixture, then into crumbs, coating well.

In a skillet, heat about 2 tablespoons oil.

Add eggplant, a few slices at a time, and saute over medium heat until golden brown on each side. Remove eggplant as it browns; add more oil as needed. Eggplant slices should be firm.

When all eggplant is browned, arrange slices, overlapping, around sides of a 3½ quart shallow baking dish or casserole; place remaining slices in bottom. Set aside, covered.

Prepare garnish: Wash tomatoes and cut each into 6 wedges.

Arrange in shallow dish; sprinkle with salt and thyme, let stand at room temperature.

About ½ hour before serving, preheat oven to 350° F.

Bake eggplant, covered, 25 minutes, or until it is piping hot. Do not overcook, or slices will become limp and soggy. (They won't taste bad, but they will not stand up around sides of casserole, which spoils the appearance of this dish.

At the same time, slowly bring beef mixture to boiling; reduce heat, and continue cooking until beef and wine are heated throughout. Turn into eggplant-lined casserole.

To serve: arrange tomato wedges, overlapping, around edge of casserole, and sprinkle with parsley. Serves 10-12.

Fondue Bourguignon

½   *pound tender steak per person, cubed. If you so desire, meat may be marinated in soy sauce and lemon juice or oil and vinegar to cover, for several hours.*
oil for cooking

Heat oil in a pot on the stove for about 10 minutes.

Transfer carefully to fondue pot.

Place meat on fondue forks and dip into oil for about 30 seconds, and eat with any of the accompanying sauces:

Bernaise Sauce

¼   *cup dry white wine*
¼   *cup white vinegar*
1   *tablespoon tarragon*
1   *tablespoon minced shallots*
   fresh ground pepper
1   *teaspoon chervil*
3   *egg yolks*
   about 1 cup melted parve margarine

Combine wine, vinegar, shallots and seasonings in a small pot.

Cook over low heat until reduced by ½. Strain and cool.

Put egg yolks into double boiler and beat until frothy with a wire whisk. Beat in vinegar mixture.

Place pan over hot but *not* boiling water (do not let boil).

Add margarine slowly, about a teaspoon at a time, beating constantly.

Be careful not to let water get too hot or it will ruin sauce.

Add additional pepper and a pinch of salt, if desired, or even additional tarragon.

Serve immediately or carefully reheat, in double boiler, just until it is luke warm.

Mustard Sauce

1 ½ cups prepared mustard
½ cup dry white wine
2 tablespoons sugar
1 teaspoon salt
2 tablespoons flour
¼ cup water

Combine mustard, wine, sugar and salt in pan. Bring to boil over medium heat, stirring constantly.

Mix flour in water, and stir into mustard mixture.

Reduce heat and simmer 10 minutes, stirring constantly.

Serve hot or cold.

Beef Wellington

One of the most impressive of all gourmet dishes. But this recipe is easy and foolproof.

3   *pounds of rib eye fillet, or middle cut shoulder*
1   *cup parve margarine*
    dash of salt
    fresh ground pepper
½   *cup each of sliced celery and onions*
1   *cup sliced carrots*
⅓   *cup chopped parsley*
1   *bay leaf*
½   *teaspoon crumbled dried rosemary*
1   *egg yolk slightly beaten and mixed with 1
    teaspoon water*
1   *recipe pastry*
1   *recipe Liver Paté*

Preheat oven to 475º F.

Spread the meat generously with margarine and sprinkle with salt and pepper.

Place vegetables, bay leaf and rosemary on the bottom of a shallow baking pan, and place meat on top of them.

Roast, uncovered, for 15-20 minutes.

Remove roast, discard vegetables and cool completely. (This can be done in the morning).

Make paté and pastry now (see below). When paté is completely cool, spread meat with paté on top and sides. (This too can be done ahead).

Preheat oven to 450º F.

Roll pastry about ⅛" thick and divide in half. Place meat on one half of rolled pastry and cover top and sides of meat with other half.

Trim edges, moisten with water, and press together. (You may decorate with braid, leaves, flowers, etc. made from leftover pastry.)

Place in baking dish and brush with yolk and water mixture. Prick crust in a few places.

Bake for about 15-20 minutes.

Remove from oven, let cool 5 minutes, slice and serve. Beef will be medium rare. Serves 6.

Liver Paté for Beef Wellington

This liver spread also makes a nice appetizer when served on lettuce with crackers or small breads. Good hot or cold.

> 1 *pound chicken livers - broiled*
> 2-3 *tablespoons parve margarine*
> 2 *tablespoons sherry*
> *pinch of thyme*
> *pinch of rosemary*
> 6 *tablespoons parve margarine or schmaltz*
> *salt and pepper to taste*

In a skillet saute the livers in the 2-3 tablespoons of margarine for about 2 minutes, or until the livers are browned.

Add the onions and the 2 tablespoons sherry, the thyme and rosemary, and cook the mixture until the onions are soft.

Puree the mixture in a blender, about ⅓ at a time.

Stir in the schmaltz or margarine and stir to mix well. If you so desire you can add 2 more tablespoons sherry or brandy.

This can be made ahead.

Pastry for Beef Wellington

> 4 *cups all purpose flour*
> ½ *pound chilled parve margarine, cut into bits*
> 6 *tablespoons vegetable shortening, chilled*
> *pinch of salt*
> 10-12 *tablespoons ice water*

In a chilled, large bowl, combine the flour, butter, shortening and salt.

Quickly, using the fingertips, blend the flour, butter and shortening together until they resemble bits of coarse meal.

At one time, pour the 10 tablespoons water over the mixture, mix together lightly, and gather the mixture into a ball. Flatten quickly with the heel of your hand, and gather mixture back into a ball.

If the dough is crumbly, add the additional water, drop by drop.

Then divide the dough in half, sprinkle with a little flour, and wrap, individually in wax paper.

Refrigerate until firm, about 2-3 hours before using it in the recipe.

Stir-Fried Beef and Vegetables

Stir frying, which has recently become fashionable in certain cooking circles, is a quick cooking technique which employs a wok and a minimal amount of cooking oil, thus making it very appealing for weight watchers and for those who like to prepare company dishes with little time and effort.

1 ½   *pounds flank steak or*
      eye-round sliced paper thin
      Peanut oil
  2   *pounds fresh spinach, chopped*
  1   *can bamboo shoots, drained*
  ½   *pound fresh mushrooms, sliced*
      any other desired vegetables

Marinade:

  ¼   *cup soy sauce*
      dash MSG (optional)
  ½   *teaspoon powdered ginger (optional)*
  2   *garlic cloves, finely chopped*

Sauce:

      left over marinade
  1   *teaspoon cornstarch*
  1   *teaspoon soy sauce*
  ½   *cup water*
      fresh ground pepper

Combine all ingredients in marinade and marinate meat as long as possible.

Heat 1 tablespoon oil in a wok, and carefully add meat, saving marinade, and stir until meat is browned on both sides. Repeat until all meat is cooked, and remove meat from wok.

Mix water, cornstarch, soy, pepper and any left over marinade.

Pour into wok, cook, stirring constantly, until mixture thickens. Remove and pour sauce over meat.

Add another tablespoon of oil to the wok, and when it is heated, stir in the spinach; cook for a few minutes.

Push the cooked spinach up the sides of the wok, add a little more oil, and cook the mushrooms and bamboo shoots (and any other vegetables).

Return meat and sauce to wok, and stir everything together until meat is heated through - about 2 minutes.

Serve immediately over white rice.

German

Buffet Surprise

One of our favorite party/buffet dishes. This can be made a week ahead and can sit in the refrigerator or it can be made, cooled, and frozen way ahead. Everybody loves it. (Even people like me, who do not like sauerkraut).

> 3   *pounds chuck roast or chuck steak*
> 3   *cans drained sauerkraut*
> 1   *box dark brown sugar*
> 1   *large can tomatoes, undrained*
> 1   *whole onion, peeled*
> 1   *apple, cut into slices*
>   *fresh ground pepper*

Place chuck in a large pot — at least 4 quarts.

Dump drained sauerkraut on top of meat.

Empty box of dark brown sugar into pot. On top of that pour can of tomatoes.

Place onion and pieces of apple in pot and grind pepper in over everything.

Cover pot and simmer until meat falls apart and is very tender — about 4 or 5 hours.

You end up with a sweet and sour tasting dish that will serve at least 20 at a buffet.

Blanquette de Veau

3½	pounds veal breast or shoulder, cut into 1" cubes
7	tablespoons parve margarine
1½	teaspoons salt
	fresh ground pepper
1	carrot peeled and sliced
1	onion stuck with 2 cloves
1	bay leaf
½	teaspoon thyme leaves
1½	pounds whole white onions, peeled, or 2 cans white onions
½	pound mushrooms, sliced
2	tablespoons flour
2	egg yolks
¼	cup Coffee Rich® or Rich Whip®
	chopped parsley or dill

In a heavy pan, sear veal well in 3 tablespoons margarine.

Cook, turning frequently, but do not let veal brown.

Add salt, pepper, carrot, onion, bay leaf, and thyme.

Pour in enough water to cover veal ¾ of the way up. Simmer veal, covered for 1 hour, or until tender.

Meanwhile, boil whole white onions in water to cover until tender, but do not let them get mushy. (If canned onions are used, drain well and brown them quickly in a little margarine). Keep onions warm.

Saute mushrooms in 2 tablespoons margarine until tender. Keep warm.

When meat is done, remove it from liquid, and keep warm.

Strain the stock, reserving 2¼ cups. Melt 2 tablespoons margarine in a saucepan and stir in flour. When smooth, slowly add reserved stock, and cook, stirring, until boiling point.

Cook over low heat 10 minutes.

Beat egg yolks and Coffee Rich® in a bowl, and slowly mix in a little of the hot sauce, stirring constantly to prevent yolks from curdling.

Return mixture to sauce in pan, and cook, stirring, until thickened.

Combine veal, sauce, onions and mushrooms and correct seasoning. (May be prepared ahead up to this point).

Cook 10 minutes over very low heat — do not let boil.

Serve with rice, and garnish with parsley or dill.

Serves 4-6.

Italian

Osso Bucco (Veal Shank Stew)

Another great cold weather, one pot dish that can be made ahead or frozen.

⅓	*cup flour (about) combined with salt and fresh ground pepper*
3 or 4	*veal shanks (with meat on bone) cut into 3" pieces*
3	*tablespoons olive oil*
1½	*cups coarsely chopped onions*
1½	*cups coarsely chopped carrots*
1½	*cups coarsely chopped celery*
2	*cloves garlic crushed*
1	*cup peeled and coarsely chopped tomatoes*
1½	*cups white wine*
1	*teaspoon dried basil leaves*
1	*teaspoon dried thyme*
1	*bay leaf*
3	*tablespoons chopped parsley*

Dredge veal shanks in flour mixture and shake off excess.

Heat the oil in a 3 or 4 quart pot and brown veal on all sides. Remove from pot and set aside.

In the same pot, adding more oil as necessary, add onions, carrots, celery, and garlic and saute for 5 minutes or until vegetables are soft. Add tomatoes, wine, basil, thyme, and bay leaf. Mix and stir well and bring to a boil.

Place the veal shanks back into the pot and simmer, covered, for about 2 hours. (If liquid does not cover all veal, more wine may be added.) Taste and correct seasoning by adding more salt and pepper if desired.

Just before serving, add parsley. Serve with rice.

Serves 4-6.

Lamb Chops Stuffed with Curried Chicken Livers

For lamb and liver lovers - and the rest of you too.

4   *thick lamb chops*
4   *chicken livers, chopped and broiled*
2   *shallots, chopped fine*
4   *tablespoons parve margarine*
    good pinch of curry powder
    fresh ground pepper
    salt
1   *tablespoon lemon juice*

Slit a pocket in the side of each lamb chop.

Melt margarine in a skillet and saute the shallots until soft and the livers until they are done the way you like them.

Remove livers and shallots from the skillet and mash livers until they are a smooth paste, (you can puree them in a blender if you wish), with lemon juice.

Season to taste with salt, pepper, and curry. Stir well to blend all ingredients.

Stuff this mixture into the chops and broil chops until they are done the way you like them.

If you so desire, you can pan fry the chops.

The liver mixture can be cooked and made ahead of time (even the day before) and the chops can be stuffed well in advance of cooking.

Lamb - French Style

The French tend to eat lamb slightly pink, which may be considered underdone by American standards. I suggest that you try it this way, just once, but if you still prefer your lamb well done, increase roasting time accordingly.

6-7 *pounds shoulder of lamb*
3 *pounds new potatoes, pared*
¼ *cup parve magarine*
2 *carrots, pared and diced*
1 *cup diced celery, with leaves*
1 *small onion, peeled and diced*
2 *cloves garlic, peeled and crushed*
dash thyme
2 *bay leaves*
¾ *cup red wine*
salt
fresh ground pepper

Preheat oven to 500° F.

Place lamb flat, fat side down in shallow roasting pan.

Arrange potatoes around meat, and dot with margarine.

Roast uncovered, 20 minutes.

Reduce oven temperature to 400° F. Turn lamb, and turn potatoes.

Sprinkle carrots, celery, onion, thyme, bay leaves and garlic over and around lamb. Roast, turning potatoes occasionally, 35-40 minutes longer; lamb will be medium rare.

Remove lamb and potatoes to serving platter; keep warm.

Pour drippings into 1 cup measure, leaving vegetables in pan. Skim off all fat and discard.

Return remaining drippings to pan, and add ½ cup water, the wine, salt and pepper.

Place pan over burner, and bring to boiling. Lower heat and simmer, uncovered, 3 minutes. Discard bay leaves.

Press vegetables and juice through a strainer into a gravy boat. Pour some of the gravy directly on the lamb (after it has been sliced) and potatoes, pass the rest.

Serves 8.

Marinated Lamb

This is one for lamb haters. I have served this to 5 known lamb-haters who swore they were eating steak. The longer this marinates, the better it gets, so I now start marinating it three days before serving. I marinate at room temperature during the day, and refrigerate it overnight, taking it out to marinate at room temperature during the day.

6-7 *pounds shoulder of lamb, boned, trimmed of fell and fat*

Marinade:

⅔ *cup olive oil*
3 *tablespoons lemon juice*
salt
fresh ground pepper
3 *tablespoons chopped parsley*
1 *teaspoon dried oregano*
3 *bay leaves, crumbled*
1 *cup thinly sliced onions*
4 *garlic cloves, thinly sliced*

In a large shallow dish or pan, combine olive oil, lemon juice, salt, pepper, parsley, oregano and bay.

Add onions and garlic.

Lay the meat in this and spoon some of the marinade over the meat.

Let meat marinate at room temperature for at least 24 hours turning every few hours.

Preheat broiler or let coals in charcoal grill get hot enough to cook on.

Without drying meat off, place it on a rack about 4″ below heat in broiler or on grill rack. Sprinkle with salt and cook about 15-20 minutes. Do not baste.

Turn meat without puncturing and moisten with a little marinade, and sprinkle with a little salt. Broil about 15 more minutes.

Meat is done when it is pale pink with a dark brown crust. Carve against the grain into thin slices and place on platter.

Serves 8.

Chicken Dijon

6   *frying chicken breasts, cut into serving pieces*
¼   *cup peanut oil (approximately)*
     cayenne pepper to taste
½   *cup Dijon mustard*
1   *cup fine unseasoned bread crumbs*
6   *tablespoons melted parve margarine*

Brush the chicken pieces on top with the peanut oil, coating them thoroughly.

Sprinkle the chicken with the cayenne pepper to taste.

Place the chicken, skin side up, in a large shallow baking pan, and bake at 350⁰ F for 30 minutes.

Remove the chicken from the oven, and turn the heat up to broil.

Brush the skin side of the chicken pieces with the Dijon mustard. (Legs should be brushed on both sides.)

Sprinkle the bread crumbs on the chicken pieces. Pour the melted margarine evenly over the bread crumbs.

Broil the chicken, 6 inches from the heat, for 3 to 5 minutes, or until the coating is golden-brown. Serve.

The broiled chicken can be frozen and reheated, wrapped in foil, in a hot (400⁰ F) oven.

Serves 4.

Roast Capon with Almond Stuffing and White Wine Sauce

Next big holiday or family get-together, break with tradition and serve this tasty and elegant poultry dish.

5-6 *pound ready to cook capon*
    salt
¼ *teaspoon ginger*
    fresh ground pepper
2 *tablespoons chopped parsley*
¼ *cup margarine, melted*

Stuffing:

½ *cup parve margarine*
    liver from capon, chopped and broiled
½ *cup finely chopped onion*
½ *cup finely chopped celery*
½ *cup chopped unblanched almonds*
3 *cups toasted white bread cubes*
    salt
½ *teaspoon dried sage leaves*
¼ *teaspoon nutmeg*

White Wine Sauce:

1 *cup boiling water*
¼ *cup light raisins*
2 *tablespoons flour*
1½ *cups chicken broth*
    salt
½ *cup white wine*

Rinse and dry capon; rub inside with salt and ginger.

Make Stuffing: In a medium skillet melt ½ cup margarine and saute liver, onions, celery and almonds for about 5 minutes, stirring.

In a large bowl, lightly toss sauteed vegetable mixture and bread cubes and rest of stuffing ingredients. Mix well. Use to lighly fill (do not pack) the neck and body cavities of the capon.

Preheat oven to 400° F.

Truss capon and place breast side up, on rack in shallow open roasting pan. Brush with some of the melted margarine.

Roast uncovered, for 20 minutes.

Reduce oven temperature to 325° F.

Roast 2 hours longer, or until nicely browned. During last ½ hour of roasting brush with remaining melted margarine.

Meanwhile, start making white wine sauce: Pour boiling water over raisins in small bowl; let stand 15 minutes; drain.

Remove capon to warm serving platter; keep warm.

Pour off drippings from roasting pan. Return 2 tablespoons drippings to pan.

Stir in flour to make smooth mixture; gradually stir in chicken broth; add salt.

Bring to a boil, stirring to dissolve browned bits in pan. Add raisins and wine.

Reduce heat; simmer, stirring 5 minutes longer, or until sauce is thickened and smooth.

Serves 6.

Chinese

Glazed Chicken

1   *3 pound roasting chicken*
1   *9-ounce crushed pineapple, undrained*
2   *tablespoons lemon juice*
2   *tablespoons prepared mustard*
1   *cup dark brown sugar*
     salt
     fresh ground pepper

On the day before roasting, mix together in a small bowl the crushed pineapple, lemon juice, mustard and brown sugar. Refrigerate this glaze until needed.

Preheat oven to 350°F.

Place chicken in the roasting pan. Sprinkle with salt and pepper. Using a pastry brush, generously "paint" the chicken with pineapple glaze.

Cover and bake about 1-1½ hours at 350° F, or until fork tender. Paint the chicken every 20 minutes.

Paella

This recipe, since it is kosher, is as close to the "real thing" as one can get. A great one-pot dish to serve to company.

    2   3-pound chickens cut into serving pieces
    ½   cup olive oil, approximately (no other)
    2   onions finely chopped
    1   clove garlic, finely chopped
    3   cups long grain raw rice
    ½   pound salami cut into thin slices or diced
    2   ripe tomatoes, peeled and chopped
    1   bay leaf
         salt
         fresh ground pepper
         pinch of saffron
    6   cups boiling water
    1   can green peas, drained
    1   can green beans, drained
         black and green pitted olives

Wash and dry chicken pieces, season with salt.

Heat ¼ cup olive oil in a large pan, and when hot, saute chicken with onions and garlic until golden brown. Remove from pan, keep warm.

Preheat oven to 325° F.

In the same pan, using more oil, combine salami, tomatoes, bay leaf, salt and pepper.

Add rice and saffron and pour boiling water over all, and stirring constantly, bring to boiling. Remove from heat.

Pour into paella pan, wok, or oven-proof au gratin.

Arrange chicken, vegetables on top. Set pan on floor of oven, or lowest rack, if oven is electric. Bake, uncovered, 25-30 minutes or until all liquid is absorbed and rice is tender. *Do not stir* after pan goes into oven.

When done, remove from oven, remove bay leaf, garnish with olives, and serve.

Serves 6.

Chicken, Normandy Style

Whenever you see the modifiers "Normandy" or "Rouenais" to describe a dish, you can be reasonably assured that brandy or cognac is one of the ingredients because the Normandy region (and Rouen, a city within it) is famous for its brandy.

½	*cup parve margarine*
1	*3-pound broiler-fryer, cut in 8 pieces*
2	*medium onions, peeled and sliced thin*
	salt
	fresh ground pepper
2	*tablespoons flour*
1½	*teaspoon curry powder (up to 1 tablespoon - to taste)*
1	*cup Coffee Rich®*
⅓	*cup brandy or cognac*

Melt margarine in heavy skillet, and add chicken pieces, onion, salt and pepper.

Cook chicken over low heat, tightly covered, for about 30 minutes, or until it is fork-tender.

Transfer chicken to a heated platter and keep warm.

Combine flour and curry powder, and add this mixture to the margarine and onions remaining in the skillet.

Stir with a whisk until smooth, and cook for a minute or two.

Stir in the Coffee Rich® and the brandy, and cook the sauce over low heat, stirring constantly, until sauce is thickened.

Return the chicken to the sauce, and simmer gently for about 10 minutes.

Serve the chicken with sauce over steamed rice.

Serves 4-6.

Suggested accompaniments: a green salad, and dry white wine.

Chinese Walnut Chicken

A great, easy, and economical company dish that can be made ahead and can be "stretched" to "feed an army."

1½-2   *pounds uncooked, boned chicken breasts cut into small bite size pieces*
2   *tablespoons cornstarch*
2   *tablespoons white sherry*
3   *tablespoons soy sauce*
1   *cup chopped walnuts*
1   *large can water chestnuts, sliced*
1   *pound fresh mushrooms, sliced*
1-2   *cans bamboo shoots, drained well*
1½   *cups celery sliced on the diagonal*
1   *cup chopped onions*
2   *cups fresh or 3 cups well drained bean sprouts*
⅓   *cup chicken broth*
   peanut oil for cooking
   fresh ground pepper
   salt

Combine cornstarch, soy sauce and sherry and stir with a whisk to remove all lumps.

Marinate chicken in this mixture for at least 2 hours, if possible.

Heat a tablespoon or two of oil in a wok (a chinese cooking utensil) and add onions and celery. Stir continuously (this is stir-frying) until vegetables are bright and translucent, but still crisp (about 2 or 3 minutes).

Push these cooked vegetables up the sides of the wok or transfer to a large bowl. (This step is repeated until everything is cooked, and to avoid repeating it, I will use an asterisk [*]).

Add another tablespoon of oil, heat, and stir-fry water chestnuts and bamboo shoots for about 2 minutes.

Add more oil, heat, and stir-fry bean sprouts and walnuts, for about 2 or 3 minutes.*

Heat a little more oil and stir-fry mushrooms until they just begin to get soft.*

Add another 2 tablespoons of oil, heat, and saute chicken pieces until done — only about 3-5 minutes. (Pieces turn beige or white when done).

Return everything to the wok and stir to mix well. Sprinkle with fresh ground pepper and salt. (Chicken can be made ahead to this point).

To finish up this recipe or to reheat, make a well in the center of the wok, through all the food, and pour in chicken broth.

When broth begins to boil and steam, stir everything together until it is all reheated (the rising steam from the broth reheats the food).

Serve over hot white rice or Chinese oven rice (under accompaniments in this book),

Serves 6 easily.

Mediterranean

Chicken Pitas

6-12	Pita Breads
3	tablespoons parve margarine
1	onion, chopped
2	tomatoes, peeled and chopped
2-3	mild peppers, chopped
2½	cups chicken, cooked and sliced thin
	fresh ground salt
½	head of lettuce, shredded

In a skillet, melt the margarine over medium heat. Add the tomatoes, and cook, stirring, for about 4 minutes.

Add the chicken, peppers, and salt. Mix well.

Warm the bread to soften them. Place some of the filling in each Pita.

Serve with lettuce sprinkled with a little oil and vinegar.

Avocado slices made a nice accompaniment to this recipe.

Serves 6 or 12.

Polynesian Chicken

   3   *broiler-fryers cut into quarters*
   ¾   *cup soy sauce*
   1   *clove garlic, crushed*
   1   *batch sweet and sour sauce (see below)*
   3   *cans (1 pound size) fruits for salad*

The day before serving, preheat oven to 350⁰ F.

Wash chicken pieces and dry well with paper towels. Arrange skin side up in large, shallow roasting pan. Drain fruit, reserving syrup.

Pour syrup and soy sauce over chicken. Add garlic. Bake uncovered basting often and turning chicken so that all pieces brown, 1 hour, or until chicken is rich, golden brown.

Make Sweet and Sour sauce:

   2   *tablespoons oil*
   2   *cups pineapple juice*
   6   *tablespoons cornstarch*
   2   *tablespoons soy sauce*
   6   *tablespoons vinegar*
 12   *tablespoons water*
   1   *cup water*
   1   *can pineapple chunks, drained*
   4   *green peppers cut into strips*

In a saucepan add pineapple juice to oil and cook over low heat for a few minutes.

Add mixture of cornstarch, soy, vinegar, water and sugar. Cook until juice thickens, stirring constantly. Add pineapple chunks and pepper strips. (This can be made ahead.)

Pour liquid from chicken into large saucepan.

Cover chicken (leave in roasting pan) tightly with foil. Add sweet and sour sauce to liquid; bring to boiling over medium heat. Continue boiling until sauce thickens and is reduced to about 3½ cups — about 45 minutes. Pour over chicken.

Refrigerate, covered, overnight. Cover drained fruit and refrigerate.

Next day, about 1½ hours before serving, preheat oven to 350⁰ F.

Bake chicken, uncovered, and basting often, for 30 minutes.

Add fruit and bake, basting several times, 30 minutes longer, or until piping hot.

To serve: Arrange chicken pieces around edge of large serving platter, around a bed of steamed white rice. Pour sauce and fruits over all.

Serves 12.

French

Poulet Marengo

Supposedly this dish was composed for Napoleon to celebrate one of his victories.

1	*3 pound chicken cut into serving pieces*
2	*tablespoons olive oil (or more)*
1	*garlic clove, peeled*
2	*onions, finely chopped*
3	*tomatoes peeled and chopped*
½-1	*pound fresh mushrooms, whole*
1	*6-ounce can tomato paste*
⅔	*cup dry white wine*
	fresh ground pepper
	pinch of parsley
	pinch of thyme
	salt

Wash and dry chicken.

Heat oil in a large dutch oven or flameproof casserole.

Add garlic clove, and discard it when it browns.

Add chicken pieces to hot oil and saute until brown on all sides.

Add more oil if necessary, and when hot, add onions, tomatoes, mushrooms and tomato paste, wine and spices.

Bring to the boil, reduce heat, and simmer covered for about 1 hour or until chicken is tender.

If sauce is too thin, stir a little flour into a bowl with a little sauce and when smooth, stir into pot, and simmer 5 more minutes.

Serves 6.

Great with noodles, French bread and white wine.

Chicken Kiev

6   *whole chicken breasts, skinned and boned and cut in half*
    about 1 cup flour
3   *well beaten eggs*
1   *cup dry bread crumbs*
    oil or shortening for frying

Herb Butter:

¾   *cup soft parve margarine*
    dash of salt
    fresh ground pepper
1   *tablespoon chopped parsley*
    pinch of rosemary
1   *teaspoon tarragon*
½   *teaspoon garlic powder*

In a small bowl make herb butter by combining parve margarine and spices. This can be done by a mix master if you so desire.

Mix well and place herb butter on a piece of wax paper and press into a flat square. Wrap and freeze.

Flatten each chicken breast carefully by placing it between 2 sheets of wax paper and pounding it with a mallet, or rolling pin, until it is thinner. Try not to break up or tear meat.

Remove herb butter from freezer and cut a small piece for each chicken breast, about 1" long by ¼" wide.

Place one piece in the middle of each chicken breast and bring the sides of the breast over butter, and fold ends over, and secure with toothpicks. Make sure no butter shows.

Roll chicken breasts in flour, then dip them in beaten eggs, and roll in bread crumbs.

When all pieces are coated, refrigerate, covered, until well chilled — about 1 hour.

In a heavy skillet, heat the oil or shortening to 375º F. Add the chicken and fry until golden brown on all sides. Drain well on paper towels.

Try not to pierce chicken while frying, and turning, or herb butter will leak out.

Serves 6.

Soyau Chicken

1 ½   cups soy sauce
3   cups water
1   cup dark brown sugar
2   tablespoons honey
1   tablespoon dry sherry
4   whole chicken breasts, skinned and boned

In a large kettle, combine the soy sauce, water, sugar, honey and the sherry.

Slowly cook this mixture over medium heat for 10 minutes; then turn the heat up, and bring the mixture to a boil.

Meanwhile, cut the chicken breats into strips about 2 to 3 inches long and 1 ½ inches wide.

Add the chicken pieces to the sauce; cover the kettle, reduce the heat, and simmer the mixture for about 30 minutes, or until the chicken is tender.

Serve the chicken in the sauce, hot or cold, with boiled white rice.

Serves 6 to 8.

Coq Au Vin

6   tablespoons parve margarine
2   tablespoons oil
3   pounds chicken cut into serving pieces
    salt
    fresh ground pepper
¼   cup cognac
3   cups red wine
1-2 cups beef bouillon (enough to cover chicken)
1   tablespoon tomato paste
2   cloves garlic, finely minced
    pinch of thyme
1   bay leaf
1   can small white onions, drained
1   pound fresh mushrooms
3   tablespoons flour
2   tablespoons parve margarine
    parsley

In a large casserole, heat oil and margarine.

Brown the chicken pieces, add mushrooms and onions, salt and pepper, cover and cook over medium heat for about 10 minutes, turning the chicken once.

Uncover chicken and add the cognac. Carefully ignite the cognac with a match and shake the casserole back and forth for a few seconds until the flame goes down.

Add the wine and just enough bouillon to cover the chicken. Stir in the tomato paste, garlic and spices.

Bring to the boil, reduce heat to simmer, cover casserole and cook slowly for 25-30 minutes.

When chicken is done, remove from pot, and skim off any fat from the cooking liquid.

Bring liquid to a boil and cook until reduced to about 2½ cups. Taste and adjust seasoning. Remove from heat and remove bay leaf.

In a small bowl combine the flour and margarine together into a smooth paste. Using a whisk, stir this into the hot cooking liquid, bringing the liquid to simmer.

Simmer and stir for a few minutes, until sauce is thick enough to coat a wooden spoon.

Replace chicken, onions and mushrooms. Sprinkle parsley over the top and serve.

This can be made ahead and reheated or frozen.

French

Fish Provencale

6	*tablespoons olive oil*
2	*cloves garlic, finely chopped*
1	*shallot, finely chopped*
1 ½	*pounds halibut or haddock in bite size pieces*
1	*teaspoon lemon juice*
2	*medium ripe tomatoes, skinned, seeded and chopped*
	salt
	fresh ground pepper
¼	*cup finely chopped parsley*

Peel tomatoes by spearing stem end with fork and placing in boiling water for about 20 seconds. Then remove skin and seeds, and chop.

Heat olive oil in heavy skillet, and saute garlic and shallot in it until tender but not browned.

Turn up heat and add the fish. Saute until lightly browned or done — do not overcook. It only takes a few minutes.

Add remaining ingredients, and cook just long enough to heat through.

Serves 4.

Suggested accompaniments: Rice is the obvious accompaniment. Tossed salad, French bread, and a nice wine will go nicely too.

Fish Supreme

2 pounds halibut or haddock
¼ cup margarine
  salt
  fresh ground pepper
1 small onion, peeled and sliced
½ lemon
¼ cup all purpose flour
  dash cayenne
2 cups table cream
¼ cup tomato paste
2 teaspoons Worcestershire sauce
4 cups hot cooked white rice
1 bay leaf
1 tablespoon chopped parsley
¼ cup dry white wine

In a large saucepan, heat 1 quart water with salt and pepper and any herbs (such as bay leaf, thyme, parsley, you wish to use), the onion and lemon.

When mixture is boiling, add raw fish. Cook about 5 minutes or until fish is tender and done. Do not overcook.

Drain, cool and refrigerate fish until ready to use.

Melt margarine in a medium saucepan. Remove from heat and stir in flour and seasonings, stirring with a whisk, until smooth.

Gradually add cream, tomato paste, Worcestershire and bay leaf. Return to heat and bring to boiling, stirring constantly.

Reduce heat, and simmer for a minute.

Stir in wine, cooked fish — broken into bite size pieces, and cook over low heat, stirring occassionally until fish is heated through — about 5 minutes. Remove bay leaf.

To serve: spoon rice around edge of serving platter   and spoon fish mixture in center. Sprinkle with parsley.

Serves 6-8.

Salmon Avocado Boats

2 cans (7¾ ounces each) red salmon
2 ripe avocados
2 teaspoons lemon juice
½ cup mayonnaise
½ teaspoon dill weed
½ teaspoon garlic salt
2 teaspoons toasted sesame seeds

Drain the salmon, removing the skin and bones.

Cut the avocados in half, and remove the seeds. Place the halves in a serving dish, and sprinkle with the lemon juice.

In a small bowl, combine the mayonnaise, dill weed, garlic salt, and the sesame seeds.

Fold in the salmon, and spoon the mixture into the avocado halves.

If not serving right away, keep the dish refrigerated.

Serves 2 to 4.

Fish in White Wine Sauce

1½-2 pounds fish (haddock or halibut)
½ cup dry white wine or vermouth
½ teaspoon thyme leaves
1 bay leaf
1 tablespoon parsley
fresh ground pepper (or 1 tablespoon peppercorns)
salt
6 tablespoons butter
¼ cup onion, finely chopped
¼ pound mushrooms, fresh, sliced
⅓ cup flour
½ cup table cream
½ cup milk
1 cup Swiss cheese, finely grated
½ cup plain bread crumbs

In a medium saucepan, combine fish, wine, ½ cup water, thyme, bay leaf, parsley, pepper, and salt and bring to a boil. Cover, reduce heat and simmer excatly two minutes.

Remove parsley, bay leaf, and peppercorns. Discard.

Drain the cooking liquid, reserving one cup. Let fish cool. Cut fish into bite size pieces. Set aside.

Melt 4 tablespoons butter in a medium sauce pan and saute the onions and mushrooms for about 4 minutes. Remove from heat and stir well until thoroughly combined.

Gradually stir in the reserved cooking liquid and the light (table) cream and the milk. Return pan to stove.

Preheat the broiler.

Bring mixture in saucepan to the boil, stirring constantly. Reduce the heat and simmer, stirring frequently, until quite thick — about five minutes.

Add grated cheese and stir until cheese is melted. Remove from heat.

Carefully stir in the fish and place in a buttered au gratin or buttered individual oven-proof dishes.

Combine bread crumbs with 2 tablespoons melted butter and sprinkle over the fish mixture. Broil 4″ from the heat in the broiler until golden brown — about two minutes.

Serve at once.

Makes 8 first course or 4 main dish servings.

Mediterranean

Baked Avocados with Fish

A nice luncheon dish or first course for a large dinner party.

3	*firm avocados*
6	*tablespoons garlic vinegar*
2	*tablespoons butter*
2	*tablespoons flour*
1	*cup cream*
	salt
1½	*cups cooked fish*
	dash of Tabasco sauce
6	*tablespoons grated cheddar cheese*

Cut unpeeled avocados in half lengthwise and remove pits. Sprinkle each half with 1 tablespoon vinegar and let stand for 30 minutes.

Preheat oven to 375° F.

Melt butter and blend in flour. Scald cream in small saucepan, and add. Cook, stirring until thickened and smooth.

Add salt, fish and Tabasco. Correct seasonings.

Stuff avocados with mixture, and sprinkle each with 1 tablespoon of cheese. Bake until heated through, about 20 minutes.

Serves 6.

Quiche

Dough for Crust:

1 ½	*cups flour*
	pinch of salt
1	*stick butter*
	about 4-6 tablespoon ice water

Filling:

4	*eggs*
1 ½	*cups whipping cream*
	pinch of salt
	pinch of nutmeg
	fresh ground pepper
	dash of cayenne
1	*tablespoon softened butter*
¼	*pound grated Swiss cheese*

Place flour and salt in a large bowl. Take butter and tear it into small pieces and toss into bowl with flour and salt.

Using your fingers, toss and pinch the flour and butter, pinching the butter into flour. When mixture resembles texture of cornmeal, it is well blended. No butter should be showing.

Now, add the ice water *very slowly*, gathering the mixture into a ball and pinching it together so it holds the shape of a ball. Just add enough water to allow the dough to retain the ball shape without crumbling.

Work the ball around in your hands for a few minutes to melt the butter and bind the ball together better. If the dough does not crumble when you break the ball in half, you have enough water. If it is still crumbly, add a little more water, but only enough to bind the dough together.

Flatten ball with your hand to get air out, gather it together, wrap in wax paper or foil, and refrigerate for an hour.

When chilled, place dough on lightly floured board and roll out from center in all directions with a rolling pin. Roll into a circle that is 2″ larger than the quiche or tart pan you are baking in.

Place dough in pan, and press against the pan. Double the edges by bringing excess dough back over the edge. Crimp or flute edge.

Fill with desired filling and bake, or cover and freeze. If you are freezing the crust, do not defrost it before using it, just remove it from the freezer, fill it, and bake it.

Filling: Preheat oven to 425° F.

Combine eggs, cream, salt, nutmeg, pepper, and cayene. Beat well to blend.

Add cream, and continue beating for a minute or two. Add all but 2 tablespoons of the cheese. Stir well.

Pour into prepared pastry (crust). Sprinkle top with 2 tablespoons of cheese and dot with butter.

Bake 25-28 minutes, or until top is lightly browned and a knife inserted in center comes out clean.

To serve: Cut into wedges.

Serves 6-8.

If perchance any is leftover, it is great cold the next day and has a completely different taste and texture.

Quiche makes a great luncheon dish with a salad, an elegant appetizer, or even can be used as a brunch entree.

Mushroom Quiche

Another great quiche — this one for mushroom lovers.

Pastry for Quiche — use preceeding recipe
    4   tablespoons butter
    2   tablespoons shallots, finely minced
    1   pound fresh mushrooms, thinly sliced
  1 ½   teaspoon salt
    1   teaspoon lemon juice
    4   eggs
    1   cup whipping cream
         fresh ground pepper
         dash nutmeg
    2   ounces grated Swiss cheese
    2   tablespoons butter, softened

Preheat oven to 350° F.

Make pastry following directions for plain quiche and fit pastry into quiche or tart pan. Chill.

Melt butter, add shallots and cook for a minute.

Stir in mushrooms, 1 teaspoon salt and lemon juice. Cover pan and simmer on low heat for 10 minutes.

Uncover pan, increase heat, and boil for 5-10 minutes, stirring frequently until liquid is evaporated and mushrooms begin to saute in butter.

Rub bottom of chilled pastry shell with 1 tablespoon of softened butter.

In a large bowl, beat eggs and cream together. Add remaining salt, pepper, and nutmeg. Stir in mushrooms.

Pour into prepared shell. Sprinkle top with cheese and dots of remaining butter.

Bake 35 minutes, or until quiche is puffy and browned and a knife inserted in center comes out clean. Serve immediately.

Serves 6-8.

Picadillo

Has numerous uses: as a filling for empanadas, enchiladas, tacos, tamales and green peppers to name just a few, or serve over rice or noodles.

2	*pounds ground beef*
3	*tablespoons olive oil*
1	*cup onions, chopped*
¼	*teaspoon finely chopped garlic clove*
3	*tomatoes, peeled, seeded, and coarsely chopped*
2	*cooking apples, peeled, cored, and coarsely chopped*
3	*canned jalapeno chilies, drained, rinsed in cold water, seeded and cut crosswise into ⅛" thick slices*
⅔	*cup seedless raisins*
10	*pimento-stuffed green olives, cut in half*
½	*teaspoon ground cinnamon*
⅛	*teaspoon ground cloves*
	fresh ground pepper
	fresh ground salt
½	*cup blanched slivered almonds*

In a heavy skillet, heat 2 tablespoons olive oil over high heat until it is hot. Add the ground meat and cook, stirring constantly. Break up any lumps in the meat.

When no sign of pink shows in the meat, add the onions and garlic, stirring well.

Reduce the heat to medium and cook for 4 minutes, then add the tomatoes, apples, chilies, raisins, olives, cinnamon, cloves, salt and pepper. Simmer, uncovered, over low heat for about 20 minutes, stirring occasionally.

In a small skillet, heat the remaining 1 tablespoon of olive oil over medium heat, tipping the skillet to make sure the bottom of the skillet is coated evenly. Add the almonds and fry them for about 2 minutes or until they are golden brown. Do not burn them. Drain the almonds well on a paper towel.

Add the almonds to the picadillo a few minutes before serving it.

Empanadas

Empanadas are Mexican turnovers, popular in Mexico and the United States. Many kinds of fillings are used: meat, poultry, vegetables, and even sweets. They freeze beautifully and can be used for appetizers, snacks, main courses, vegetables, or desserts.

When empanadas are being used for dessert they are made in different sizes and the pastry must be sweetened.

Fillings for dessert can include any flavor jelly or jam, thick applesauce flavored with cinnamon, or any cream filling. Pie fillings can also be used or any kind of fruit preserves. Old fashioned dessert empanadas were made with pear preserves or guava jelly.

Basic Recipe for Empanadas

> 2   *cups all purpose flour measured after sifting*
> 2   *teaspoons baking powder*
>   *fresh ground salt*
> ½   *cup shortening*
>   *ice water (between ¼ and ⅓ cup approximately)*
>
> **for dessert empanadas, add 2 Tablespoons sugar to the basic empanada dough recipe*

In a large bowl, sift together the flour, baking powder, and salt. Add the shortening and work it into the flour using your thumb and first two fingers in a pinching motion. The idea is to incorporate the shortening into the flour. When done properly, the mixture will resemble coarse meal.

Slowly add the ice water, a tablespoon at a time, pinching and working the liquid into the solid. Depending on the temperature, humidity, heat in your house, time of year, etc. etc. etc. the amount of ice water required will vary — there is no set amount.

When the dough begins to hold together, gather it into a ball and knead it with your fingers for a few minutes to make sure the dough is not crumbly on the inside of the ball.

Divide the dough into 12 even pieces.

On a lightly floured board, roll out each piece and cut the dough into 4″ (in diameter) rounds. Place a spoonful of filling on one half of the round, wet the edges with water, and fold the other half over.

Be sure and press the edges firmly to seal in the filling. You can seal them further by pressing the outside edges with the tines of a table fork.

To shape the empanadas, first curve the ends to gently form a crescent (half moon). Then, using your thumb and first finger, pinch folds that overlap all around the edge.

Heat about 3″ of oil in a deep-fat fryer or heavy saucepan to about 375° F.

Fry the empanadas a few at a time until golden brown. Drain well on paper towel.

If you want to bake them, brush them with a mixture of 1 egg yolk and 1 tablespoon water, and bake them at 400°F for 15 to 20 minutes.

If making dessert empanadas, while they are still hot, dip them in a mixture of 2 cups sugar to 1 tablespoon cinnamon — or shake powdered sugar over them.

Empanadas can be made smaller or larger depending on whether you want them for cocktail accompaniments or as part of the meal.

Manicotti

A low calorie favorite company dish for a big crowd for bruch or dinner. Very light tasting and goes great with a salad.

Crepes:

1 ¼	*cups water*
5	*eggs*
1 ¼	*cups unsifted flour*
	pinch of salt

Sauce:

¼	*cup olive oil*
1	*cup finely chopped onion*
1	*crushed garlic clove*
1	*2-pound, 3 ounce can of tomatoes*
1	*6-ounce can of tomato paste*
3	*tablespoons of parsley*
2 ¼	*teaspoons sugar*
1 ½	*teaspoons oregano*
½	*teaspoon basil*
	fresh ground pepper to taste.

Filling:

2	*pounds cottage cheese*
8	*ounces diced Munster cheese*
⅓	*cup grated Swiss cheese*
2	*tablespoons parsley*
	salt
	fresh ground pepper

Blend crepe ingredients.

Heat a crepe pan on medium heat for a few minutes, brush pan with melted butter, pour in just enough batter to just cover the bottom of the pan.

Cook crepe until dry on the top and barely lightly browned on the bottom. Turn crepe and cook for a moment. Remove from pan and repeat process.

Crepes for the manicotti recipe should be almost white and not browned. Stack crepes as you make them.

In ¼ cup olive oil, saute 1 cup finely chopped onion and 1 crushed garlic clove.

Add remaining sauce ingredients, bring to boiling, cover and simmer on low for 1 hour.

Combine filling ingredients in a bowl.

To assemble manicotti, pour some of the sauce over the bottom of an au gratin or a large shallow oven-proof dish.

Fill crepes by placing approximately a tablespoon or two of the filling in the center of each crepe and folding the ends of the crepe over the filling (i.e. fold crepe in thirds).

Place filled crepe seam side down in baking pan. Cover crepes with rest of sauce, sprinkle with some grated Swiss cheese and bake at 350⁰ F for 30 minutes.

This dish makes about 30 manicotti, which should serve 8 or 10 people easily. It freezes beautifully, and should be frozen before baking it. To cook frozen manicotti, preheat oven to about 375⁰ F or 400⁰ F and place frozen manicotti in oven. When manicotti is heated through, it is ready to eat — about 30 minutes. Check and make sure they are piping hot, though.

Accompaniments

Orange Rice

½   cup celery, thinly sliced
3   tablespoons finely chopped onion
½   stick parve margarine
1½ cups water
1   cup orange juice
2   tablespoons grated orange rind
    salt
    fresh ground pepper
1   cup raw rice

In a heavy pot, saute the celery and onion in ½ stick of margarine, stirring, until the vegetables are light and translucent, about two or three minutes.

Stir in the water, orange juice, orange rind, salt and pepper.

Bring the mixture to a boil, sprinkle in the raw rice, cover pot and cook over low heat for about 20 minutes, or until rice is tender.

Great with meat or poultry.

Chinese Brown Oven Rice

This is my all time favorite vegetable and I serve it with almost every main course I make. It is the moistest rice I have ever eaten and I always receive compliments on it.

> 2 *cups long grain raw rice*
> 1 *can sliced mushrooms with juice*
> ¼ *cup oil*
> 3 *tablespoon soy sauce*
> 1 *package dry onion soup*
> *water*

Preheat oven to 350⁰ F.

Mix together the rice, oil, soy sauce, onion soup and the mushrooms — but not the mushroom juice, in a large 3 quart casserole or ovenproof dish.

Pour mushroom juice into a measuring cup, and add enough water to make one cup of liquid. Pour liquid into the casserole. Add three more cups of water. Stir well to mix.

Cover and bake for 50-60 minutes.

Serves 8.

Confetti Rice

1   cup sliced fresh mushrooms
½   cup chopped onion
⅓   cup parve margarine
3   cups cooked long grain rice
1   10-ounce package frozen peas, cooked
¼   cup slivered almonds, blanched and toasted*
1   teaspoon salt
     fresh ground pepper
¼   teaspoon rosemary leaves

Cook mushrooms and onions in melted butter over medium heat until onions are translucent, but not brown. (Mushrooms will be brown, which is okay).

Add the rice, peas and seasonings. This dish may be prepared in advance up to this point.

Heat the mixture, stirring occasionally, over medium heat until thoroughly heated; just before serving, stir in the almonds.

Serves 6.

*To blanch almonds, placed shelled almonds in boiling water for one minute; drain. When cool enough to handle, the outer skins will slide right off. With a sharp knife, cut almonds into slivers. (Freeze those that you do not need for later use.) Place slivered almonds on baking sheet and toast in slow oven 15-20 minutes.

Fettucine Alfredo

This classic noodle dish from Northern Italy is very rich and filling, and thus serves quite adequately as a main dish, accompanied by a crisp green salad and hot Italian bread.

½   *pound egg noodles, ¼" wide*
½   *cup butter*
⅔   *cup whipping cream*
1¼ *cup grated Swiss cheese*
    salt
    fresh ground pepper
    chopped parsley

In a large pot, bring 4 quarts of water with 1 tablespoon salt, to boiling. Add the noodles and cook, uncovered, until tender, about 15-20 minutes. Drain noodles, and keep warm.

Meanwhile, make Alfredo sauce: Heat butter and cream in a medium saucepan over low heat until butter is melted. Remove from heat.

Add 1 cup of the cheese, salt and pepper to taste, and stir until the sauce is blended and smooth.

Add the sauce to the drained noodles and toss with two spoons until the noodles are evenly coated.

Sprinkle with remaining cheese and chopped parsley. Serve at once.

Serves 6.

Noodle Casserole

Another great favorite that can be used as a meal in itself.

½ *pound medium size noodles*
2 *cups cottage cheese*
2 *cups sour cream*
¼ *cup butter, melted*
¼ *cup finely chopped onion*
1 *clove garlic, minced*
1 *teaspoon Worcestershire*
    dash Tobasco sauce
    salt
    fresh ground pepper

Cook noodles in 4 quarts of boiling salted water until they are moderately tender — about 10 minutes. Drain and rinse with cold water.

In a bowl combine the cottage cheese, sour cream, melted butter, chopped onion, garlic, Worcestershire, tobasco, salt and pepper.

Stir in the noodles and transfer the mixture to a buttered 2 quart baking dish or casserole.

Bake noodles, uncovered, at 350° F for 45 minutes.

Serve hot, accompanied, if you like, with grated cheese.

Serves 8.

Pommes Dauphine (Fried Potato Balls)

This is very rich, so save it for a special occasion. It goes best with a simple meat dish.

3   cups warm mashed potatoes
10   tablespoons parve margarine
¼   cup Coffee Rich® (whipping cream if to be used with dairy)
2   egg yolks lightly beaten
1¼   teaspoons salt
1   cup flour
4   eggs
     salad oil for deep frying

Combine the potatoes with 4 tablespoons butter, the cream, egg yolks and 1 teaspoon of the salt.

In a saucepan, heat 1 cup water, the remaining butter and ¼ teaspoon salt, until the butter is melted and mixture is boiling rapidly. Add the flour all at once, remove pan from the heat, and stir the flour in quickly.

Hold the pan above the heat and stir the mixture vigorously until the dough is thick and pulls away from the sides of the pan to form a ball.

Add the four eggs, one at a time, beating well after each addition.

Add the potatoes and beat them in well.

Shape the paste into balls, and deep-fry them in hot deep oil (370º F) until they are lightly browned and puffed. Drain the balls on paper towels before serving.

Spiced Acorn Squash

> 4 *medium sized acorn squash*
> ½ *cup dark brown sugar*
> 1½ *teaspoons cinnamon*
> ½ *teaspoon nutmeg*
> ¼ *teaspoon ground cloves*
> *pinch of salt*
> 8 *tablespoons melted margarine*
> ½ *cup maple syrup*
> *approximately 2 cups boiling water*

Preheat oven to 350º F.

Cut each squash in half and scoop out seeds and fibers.

In a small bowl combine sugar, spices and margarine. Stir well.

Arrange squash halves in a shallow baking dish. Spoon butter sauce into squash halves. Pour 1 tablespoon maple syrup over sauce (in squash half).

Pour boiling water into ovenproof dish until water is about 1″ deep. Place squash halves in dish.

Bake in middle oven for 30 minutes.

Serve at once.

Serves 8.

Broccoli with Lemon

Such a delightful change from ordinary ways of serving broccoli, and this dish goes with virtually anything.

  1 *bunch fresh broccoli or 2 10-ounce packages*
      frozen
 ¼ *cup olive oil*
  1 *clove garlic, minced*
  2 *tablespoons lemon juice*

If using fresh broccoli, remove leaves and tough portions. Wash thoroughly, drain, and separate, splitting larger stalks into quarters.

In a large kettle, bring 6 cups of salted water to boiling, and add fresh broccoli. (If frozen broccoli is used, cook according to package label directions.) Cook broccoli, covered, 10 minutes, or until tender. (The broccoli will start losing its brilliant green coloring when it is tender — not as pretty, but easier to chew).

Drain cooked broccoli thoroughly in colander.

In the same kettle, place olive oil and garlic, and heat until bubbly; do not let garlic brown. Add broccoli, sprinkle with lemon juice and add salt to taste.

Cook, covered, 1 minute, or until broccoli is heated through. Serve immediately.

Serves 4.

Eggplant Melange

If there are eggplant lovers in your house, they'll love this tasty dish. It goes nicely with roast lamb or beef.

1   *medium eggplant*
6   *tablespoons olive oil*
1   *pound button mushrooms, washed and trimmed*
1   *clove garlic, minced*
     oregano
     salt
     fresh ground pepper
1   *cup cooked green peas, fresh or frozen*
1   *small can Italian tomatoes*

Peel the eggplant, halve it lengthwise, and cut the halves into vertical slices about ¼" thick.

In a large skillet, heat 4 tablespoons olive oil, and when heated, saute the eggplant slices until golden. Remove eggplant, and drain on paper towels.

In the small skillet, saute the mushrooms and garlic in remaining olive oil. Season with oregano, salt and pepper to taste. Saute for about 10 minutes, or until mushrooms are tender but still firm.

Stir in the peas, the reserved eggplant and the tomatoes. Crush the tomatoes as you stir them into the mixture. (Dish may be made in advance up to this point).

Simmer the vegetables for 15 minutes; serve hot.

Serves 6.

Carrot Cake Ring

Another one of my very favorite company vegetables. Great at a buffet.

¾ cup shortening
2 eggs, separated
½ cup brown sugar
1 teaspoon lemon juice
1 tablespoon cold water
1½ cups grated carrots
1 cup sifted flour
½ teaspoon baking soda
1 teaspoon baking powder
½ teaspoon salt
 bread crumbs

Preheat oven to 375° F.

In a large bowl (of an electric mixer), cream together shortening, egg yolks and brown sugar. Beat until smooth and fluffy.

Add lemon juice, cold water, and carrots. Blend well.

Sift together flour, baking soda, baking powder, and salt and add to carrot mixture.

Beat egg whites until stiff, and fold into batter.

Grease a 9-inch ring mold and sprinkle with bread crumbs until you have a thin coat all around the mold. Shake off any excess. Pour in carrot cake batter bake 40-45 minutes.

This "cake" is a great vegetable and when unmolded you can fill the middle with cooked and drained peas mixed with mushroom slices.

Serves 8-10.

Lemon Rice

2 ½   *cups fresh or canned chicken broth*
  1   *tablespoon lemon juice*
1 ½   *teaspoons salt*
  1   *bay leaf*
  ¼   *teaspoon white pepper*
  ½   *cup margarine*
  1   *cup long grain white rice, uncooked*

In the top part of a double boiler, over direct heat, cook the chicken stock, lemon juice, salt, bay leaf, pepper, and one-half of the margarine until hot.

Stir in the rice.

Place the mixture over the bottom part of a double boiler, which should be filled with gently boiling water.

Cover the top part, and cook for 35 minutes, stirring occasionally.

Remove from the heat; remove the bay leaf, and discard it.

Just before serving, toss the rice with the remaining margarine.

Serves 4.

Breads

The following three recipes are for different varieties of fruit-and-nut breads which can also be served as cake for dessert or snacks. Regardless of what you call them - or how you serve them — they are very similar in terms of basic ingredients and method of preparation and storage. The texture of the finished products is like that of a very moist pound cake. They must be refrigerated, and in fact, they keep indefinitely when properly stored in the refrigerator or freezer. You can bake them either in loaf pans or tube pans; and, you will find that they can serve as a suitable accompaniment to brunch, as a nice dessert for a simple meal, or just as something special to serve with coffee or tea anytime.

American

Banana Bread

A good way to use up bananas that are too ripe to eat.

¾	cup shortening
1 ½	teaspoon baking powder
2	eggs, lightly beaten
3	small or 2 large very ripe bananas
2	cups all purpose flour
¾	cup walnuts, chopped
½	teaspoon baking soda
1	cup sugar
1	teaspoon salt

Preheat oven to 350⁰ F.

In a medium bowl, cream together shortening and sugar until fluffy. Add the eggs.

Sift together the dry ingredients, and add to the creamed mixture.

Mash the bananas well, and add, along with the walnuts, to the batter. Mix only until ingredients are combined; batter will be thick.

Bake in greased 9x5x3-inch loaf pan for 1 hour, or until well browned on top, and loaf tests done.

Turn loaf onto wire rack, and cool thoroughly. Then wrap in aluminum foil, and refrigerate several hours before serving.

Serves 10-12

Apricot Walnut Tea Bread

1	cup dried apricots
1½	cups boiling water
2½	cups sifted all purpose flour
3	teaspoons baking powder
½	teaspoon salt
1	egg
1	teaspoon vanilla
1	cup sugar
¼	cup salad oil
1	cup walnuts, coarsely chopped

Using a scissors, cut the dried apricots into small pieces, and place in a small bowl. Add the boiling water; set aside to cool.

Preheat the oven to 350° F.

Sift the flour, baking powder and salt together onto a sheet of waxed paper; set aside.

In a large bowl combine egg, vanilla, sugar and oil; with a wooden spoon, beat until well blended.

Gradually add apricot mixture, beating constantly.

Add flour mixture all at once; beat only until smooth; stir in nuts just until well combined.

Turn batter into a greased 9x5x3-inch loaf pan, and bake 1 hour, or until loaf tests done.

Let cool in pan on a wire rack for 10 minutes; then, carefully loosen with a spatula to remove loaf onto rack. Let cool completely. Wrap in foil and store in refrigerator at least 12 hours before slicing.

Serves 10-12.

Cranberry Bread

Prepare this tangy bread around the holiday season, when fresh cranberries are available at the supermarket. If you are ambitious, double or triple the recipe, and then you will have extras for company or to give as gifts.

2	*cups all purpose flour*
1	*cup sugar*
1 ½	*teaspoons baking powder*
½	*teaspoon baking soda*
1	*teaspoon salt*
¼	*cup shortening*
1	*tablespoon grated orange rind*
¾	*cup orange juice*
1	*egg, well beaten*
½	*cup chopped pecans*
2	*cups fresh cranberries, chopped*

Preheat oven to 350° F.

Into a large bowl, sift together all dry ingredients. Cut in the shortening until the mixture resembles coarse corn meal.

Combine orange juice, grated orange rind and egg, and add all at once to dry ingredients, mixing just enough to dampen them.

Fold in chopped pecans and cranberries, mixing just until combined.

Bake in greased 9x5x3-inch loaf pan for 1 hour, or until loaf tests done.

Cool thoroughly on wire rack, wrap in foil and refrigerate. Store overnight for easier slicing.

Serves 10-12.

Brioches

These rich English rolls are an excellent accompaniment to any egg dish, or just serve them alone with butter, jam and coffee or tea. They are a little too rich to serve with a dinner, but you may do so if you wish. They can be filled and used as an appetizer, or you can make 1 large one instead of many small, fill it and serve it for a main course. Brioches keep beautifully in the freezer indefinitely. To reheat, simply place brioches directly from freezer into a preheated hot (400º F) oven for about 10 minutes.

> 1   *package yeast*
> ½   *cup warm water*
> ¼   *cup sugar*
> 2   *teaspoons salt*
> 1   *egg yolk mixed with 1 tablespoon water*
> 1   *cup butter*
> 6   *eggs*
> 3   *cups sifted flour*
> 1½   *cups additional sifted flour*

One day before you want to serve brioches: Sprinkle one package of yeast over warm water in a large bowl; stir until yeast is dissolved.

Add sugar, salt, butter, eggs, and 3 cups flour. Beat at medium speed for 4 minutes, occasionally scraping sides of bowl and beaters with rubber scrapper.

Add 1½ cups more sifted flour. Beat at low speed 2 minutes longer, or until smooth — dough will be soft.

Cover bowl with foil (lightly oil underside to prevent sticking). Let dough rise in warm place, free from drafts, until double in bulk — about 1½-2 hours.

Using a rubber scraper, beat down dough. Then refrigerate, covered with foil, overnight.

Next day: Grease 24 3-inch muffin tin cups or special brioche tins. (If making one large brioche, use a 1 or 1½ quarts brioche tin).

Remove dough from refrigerator — it will have a spongy consistency. Turn dough onto lightly floured surface; divide in half. Return half to bowl and refrigerate until ready to use.

Working quickly, shape ¾ of the dough on the board into a 12″ roll. With a sharp knife, cut into 12 pieces.

Shape each piece into a ball; place in prepared tins.

Using the same method, divide the other ¼ of the dough on the board into 12 smaller pieces, and shape into smaller balls. Dip your thumb in flour, and press indentation in center of each of the large balls in tins.

In each indentation, place a small ball of dough. Keep your thumb well floured for this operation to prevent sticking.

Cover brioches with a towel and let them rise in a warm place until dough has doubled in bulk — about 1 hour.

Meanwhile, shape the other half of the dough in the same way, and let rise as directed.

Preheat the oven to 400° F.

Beat the egg yolk with the water. Brush on tops of each brioche.

Bake 15-20 minutes or until golden brown. Serve hot with butter and jam.

Makes at least 2 dozen brioches.

Desserts

Lemon Angel Cake

1   *angel food cake or 1 chiffon cake*
1   *small package lemon pudding and pie filling mix*
2   *tablespoons lemon juice*
1   *tablespoon grated lemon peel*
2½   *cups whipping cream (or Rich Whip®)*
2   *cans of flaked coconut*
2   *egg yolks*
½   *cup sugar*

Prepare pudding mix as package directs for lemon meringue pie, reducing the amount of water used to 2 cups.

Remove from heat and stir in lemon juice and peel.

Pour filling mixture into a medium bowl and place covered into refrigerator until cool. About 1 hour.

Split cake into 4 or 5 layers.

Whip one cup of cream and fold in 1 can of coconut. Fold cream-coconut mixture into cooled pudding filling.

Assemble cake layers by placing 1 layer on a plate and covering it with ¼ of the lemon filling.

Place another cake layer on top and repeat process. End with a layer of cake on top, as all filling should be between cake layers. Refrigerate covered overnight.

Several hours before serving, whip remaining 1½ cups of cream. Fold in the other can of coconut. Ice top and sides of cake. Keep in refrigerator until serving.

Serves 10-12.

Chocolate Mousse Cake

For fellow chocolate lovers.

Cake:

8	*egg whites*
½	*cup sifted unsweetened cocoa*
¾	*cup boiling water*
1¾	*cups sugar*
1½	*teaspoons baking soda*
1¾	*cup sifted cake flour*
	pinch of salt
½	*cup salad oil*
7	*egg yolks*
2	*teaspoons vanilla extract*
½	*teaspoon cream of tartar*

Chocolate Cream:

3	*cups whipping cream or Rich Whip*®
1½	*cups sifted confectioners' sugar*
¾	*cup unsweetened cocoa*
1½	*teaspoon vanilla*
½	*teaspoon rum*
	pinch of salt
1	*teaspoon unflavored gelatine*

Make cake: In large bowl of electric mixer, let egg whites come to room temperature.

Preheat oven to 325º F.

Place cocoa in a small bowl; add boiling water, stirring until smooth. Cool about 20 minutes.

In another large bowl, sift flour, sugar, soda and salt. Make a well in center and pour in oil, yolks, vanilla and cooled cocoa. With spoon or electric mixer, beat just until smooth.

Sprinkle cream of tartar over egg whites. Beat whites, at high speed, until very stiff.

Pour batter over egg whites; with rubber scraper gently fold into egg whites just until blended.

Turn into ungreased 10″ tube pan. Bake 60 minutes. Cool completely.

Make chocolate cream: Pour cream into a large bowl; refrigerate until very cold — about 30 minutes.

Add sugar, cocoa, vanilla, and rum. Beat until stiff enough to hold its shape. Refrigerate.

Sprinkle gelatine over 2 tablespoons cold water to soften. Heat over hot water, stirring until dissolved; let cool.

Prepare cake for filling: Cut a 1-inch slice, cross-wise from the top of the cake; set aside. With a sharp knife, outline a well in the cake, being careful to leave ¾-inch thick walls around the center holes and sides. With your fingers, or a spoon, carefully remove cake from this area, being sure to leave a 1″ thick base at bottom. Reserve 1¼ cups crumbled cake from what you have taken out.

Measure 2½ cups of chocolate cream into a small bowl; fold in cooled gelatine. Fill well you made in cake with this mixture.

Replace top of cake.

Mix ½ cup of the chocolate cream with the reserved crumbled cake. Fill hole in center of cake.

Frost top and sides of cake with remaining chocolate cream. Refrigerate until well chilled.

Serves 10-12.

Chocolate Gateau

A very rich French cake. It freezes beautifully with its frosting.
Serve only small portions or else.

2	*tablespoons dark rum*
⅔	*cup semi-sweet chocolate morsels*
1	*stick butter or parve margarine, softened*
3	*eggs, separated*
	pinch of salt
⅓	*cup pulverized blanched almonds*
¼	*teaspoon almond extract*
⅔	*cup granulated sugar*
¼	*teaspoon cream of tartar*
2	*tablespoons granulated sugar*
¾	*cup cake flour*

Preheat oven to 350⁰ F.

Rub the inside of a round 8-inch spring form pan with soft butter
and sprinkle with a little flour. Cover bottom and sides.

Carefully melt chocolate and rum in a small pan, over boiling
water (in another pan). Remove from heat, set aside.

Measure all ingredients for the rest of the cake before beginning.

Cream butter and sugar together until soft and fluffy. Beat in yolks.

In another bowl, whip egg whites with cream of tartar. Beat until
whites will hold a peak.

Add 2 tablespoons sugar and beat for another minute until they are
smooth and shiny, and hold a peak. Set aside.

Stir chocolate up and add to the butter-sugar-yolk mixture. Fold in
the almonds and almond extract and flour.

With a rubber spatula, stir in ¼ of the beaten whites to soften the
batter. Place rest of whites on top of batter and fold in, rapidly.

Place batter in prepared pan and bake for about 25 minutes. If cake
does not test done, bake a few more minutes. Top should begin to
crack and middle should be slightly moist.

Remove from oven and cool in pan for 10 minutes. Remove from
pan and cool on a rack for about 2 hours before icing.

Chocolate Icing

This icing is nothing but *rich* and *fantastic*.

½   *pound butter or parve margarine softened*
1   *pound powdered sugar*
3   *egg yolks*
3   *ounces dark sweet chocolate, melted and cooled*
1   *tablespoon rum*

Cream butter until soft.

Gradually add powdered sugar and beat well to blend.

Add yolks slowly, one at a time. Stir in cooled melted chocolate, adding a little a a time. Add rum, and beat well to blend.

Ice cake.

Serves 10-12.

Mediterranean

Heavenly Grapes

4   *cups seedless green grapes*
2   *cups sour cream*
3   *tablespoons dark brown sugar*
1 ½   *tablespoons white creme de cacao*

In a large bowl, combine all the ingredients, mixing well.

Chill the mixture for several hours, to allow the flavors to develop.

To serve, spoon the grapes and their sauce into 6 to 8 champagne or wine glasses.

Serves 6 to 8.

NOTE: fresh peaches, peeled and sliced, may be substituted for the grapes.

Cherry Tart

2   1 pound cans sour red pitted cherries (drain
    and save liquid)
1   cup sugar
2   tablespoons Kirsch — optional but preferred
2   cups flour
    salt
⅔   cup butter or parve margarine
1   egg slightly beaten
¼   teaspoon almond extract
2   teaspoons grated lemon rind
4   teaspoons cornstarch

Sprinkle cherries with ⅔ cup sugar and Kirsch. Let stand 1 hour.
Preheat oven to 350⁰ F.

Make dough by sifting flour and remaining ⅓ cup sugar and salt.

Cut in butter (in small pieces) and make "fine meal" by working
butter and flour together with your fingers.

Make a well in the center of the dry ingredients and add eggs,
water and lemon rind. Work flour and liquid together, until dough
will stick and form a ball.

Turn out onto a lightly floured board. Using the heel of your hand,
knead 3 or 4 times. Reshape dough into a ball, wrap in wax paper,
chill for ½ hour.

Then pat pastry into a round 9-inch slip-bottom pan, pressing
dough evenly over bottom and sides of pan. Crimp dough to make
an edge.

Drain cherries well, reserving liquid.

Add enough liquid from the can of cherries to measure one cup,
and add to a saucepan containing the cornstarch. Stir in liquid and
bring to a boil, stirring and simmering 2-3 minutes until liquid is
clear thick. Add to cherries.

Add extract and mix gently. Pour into tart shell.

Bake 50 minutes until crust is golden and filling is bubbly. Serve
warm or cold with whipped cream.

Serves 8.

French Apple Tart

Use pastry from Cherry Tart recipe.

2   *pounds cooking apples, peeled and cored —*
    slice two apples and save for topping
2   *tablespoons water*
4   *ounces sugar*
1   *ounce butter or parve margarine*
    grated rind of 1 small orange
2   *tablespoons apricot jam*
2   *tablespoons water*
1   *teaspoon lemon juice*

Cook apples with water in a covered pan until tender.

Add sugar and butter and grated orange rind. Cook uncovered stirring occasionally until you have a thick puree. Remove pan from heat, cool filling.

Preheat oven to 400⁰ F.

Roll out pastry and place in an 8½-inch or 9-inch quiche or tart pan. Fill with cold apple puree. Placed sliced apples over top.

Bake at 400⁰ F for 25-30 minutes.

To make glaze: Heat apricot jam, lemon juice, and water until syrupy. Glaze tart after cooking.

Serves 8.

Trifle

A great Passover treat that can be made a day ahead and feeds an army. At Passover the custard would have to be left out unless you are serving a dairy meal. Trifle is a great dessert to use any time of the year though.

    2   *9-inch sponge cakes broken up or one large cake*
        broken up.
    2   *packages (10 ounce) frozen raspberries thawed*
        and drained (save liquid)
    2   *cans peaches, drained (save liquid)*
    1   *large can fruit cocktail drained (save liquid)*
        optional: ¾ cup dry sherry mixed with all the
        liquids from the fruits
 1½   *cups whipped cream or Rich Whip® (whipped*
        just before assembling this dessert)
    2   *cans shredded coconut*
    8   *ounces slivered almonds*
        chilled custard sauce

Custard sauce:

    2   *cups milk*
    ¼   *cup sugar*
    1   *teaspoon vanilla*
    6   *egg yolks*
        pinch of salt

If making or using custard: Scald milk in a double boiler.

Beak yolks, add sugar and salt. Pour a little hot milk into yolks and beat, and then add the rest of the milk.

Place over medium heat and cook, stirring constantly until mixture is thick enough to coat a wooden spoon.

Pour into a bowl and stir in vanilla. Cover and refrigerate for about 1 hour. Custard will *not* be very thick.

To assemble: place some of the cake in the bottom of a large attractive glass or crystal serving dish, bowl or brandy snifter. Sprinkle with juice-sherry mixture; cake pieces should be fairly well saturated.

Combine all fruits, and place some on top of cake pieces. Top this with some of the custard, then whipped cream, coconut and almonds. Repeat until everything is used up. Refrigerate.

Serves 12-14 easily.

Chocolate Fudge Roll

  6   *eggs, separated*
 ¾   *cup sugar*
  1   *cup (6 ounces) semisweet chocolate chips*
 ¼   *cup water*
 ¼   *cup unsweetened cocoa*
  1   *pint heavy cream*

Preheat the oven to 350° F.

In a large bowl, with an electric mixer at medium speed, beat the egg yolks and sugar until thick and lemon-colored — about 5 minutes.

In the top part of the double boiler, over hot water, melt the chocolate with the water; remove from the heat and let cool.

When chocolate has cooled, add it to the egg yolk mixture.

Throughly wash the beaters, and in a deep bowl, with an electric mixer at high speed, beat the egg whites until stiff; fold them into the chocolate mixture.

Grease an 11x17-inch jelly roll pan and cover it with waxed paper; grease and lightly flour the waxed paper. Spread the batter evenly around the pan and bake it for 20 minutes.

Remove the pan from the oven and cover the cake with a damp cloth for 15 minutes.

Place another damp cloth on a flat surface and cover it with a piece of waxed paper about 11x17 inches. Sprinkle the cocoa evenly over the waxed paper.

Invert the cake onto the waxed paper covered with cocoa. Carefully peel off the waxed paper that the cake was baked with.

In a large bowl, with an electric mixer at high speed, whip the cream just until soft peaks form.

Spread three-fourths of the whipped cream over the cake to within 1 inch of the outside edges.

Roll the cake up lengthwise, removing the waxed paper as you roll. Ice the cake with the remaining whipped cream.

If desired, garnish the top with a little grated chocolate.

Refrigerate the cake until serving.

Serves 10 to 12.

Crepes

1 ½   cups milk (or water)
3   eggs
1 ½   cups all purpose flour
1   tablespoon sugar
1   teaspoon melted butter

Pour milk or water, flour, eggs, sugar, and melted butter into a blender or beat by hand until smooth and blended. If possible let batter stand at room temperature for 2 hours.

Heat a crepe pan on medium heat for about 5 minutes. Brush pan with melted margarine.

Add just enough batter to barely cover bottom of pan. Brown crepe lightly on one side, turn over and brown lightly on the other side. Remove from pan.

Repeat process, adding melted margarine as needed.

Strawberry Filling (For Crepes)

1   quart fresh or frozen strawberries, hulled and halved
¼   cup sugar
3   tablespoons Kirsch
3   tablespoons currant jelly
2   tablespoons water
    optional: whipped cream or Rich Whip® — whipped with a little sugar and vanilla

Place berries, sugar, Kirsch, jelly and water in a deep skillet.

Heat slowly and bring to a boil, turn down and simmer, covered, for about 3 minutes.

Place 2-3 tablespoons of this mixture in a crepe, roll crepe closed. Lay filled crepes in serving dish, seam side down.

Fill all crepes and place in serving dish. Place a big spoonful of whipped cream on top of every crepe.

Makes about 14 crepes, depending on size of crepe.

Gateau des Crepes

Approximately 20 crepes of 8 or 9-inch diameter — use preceeding recipe.

> 2 *pounds tart apples*
> 2 *tablespoon butter or parve margarine*
> 1 *cup sugar*
> ¼ *cup Calvados or apple juice*
> 1½ *cups slivered almonds*

Meringue:

> 2 *egg whites*
> ¼ *teaspoon cream of tartar*
> ¼ *cup sugar*

Peel, core and chop the apples.

Melt butter in a large, heavy pot with a tight fitting lid.

Add apples and toss to coat with butter. Cook, covered, over low heat, stirring occasionally until apples are soft, about ½ hour.

Stir in 1 cup sugar and the Calvados or apple juice. Cook, uncovered, stirring frequently for about 5 minutes over medium heat.

Spread about 2-3 tablespoons of the apple mixture on 1 crepe. Place this crepe on a buttered dish or cookie sheet.

Sprinkle about 1 tablespoon of almonds on top of apple mixture on crepe. Place another crepe on top and repeat.

Dessert may be made ahead to this point. Refrigerate if making ahead.

Before serving, preheat oven to 400° F and make meringue by beating egg whites and cream of tartar until foamy.

Add sugar, a tablespoon full at a time, until you have a stiff meringue.

Ice gateau of crepes with meringue as you would a cake.

Bake at 400° F for 5-7 minutes.

Serves 8-10.

Cold Chocolate Souffle

A great favorite of ours for company.

2   *envelopes unflavored gelatin*
½   *cup orange juice*
1   *6-ounce package semisweet chocolate bits*
¼   *cup strong coffee* or *½ cup strong coffee and* no *Kahlua*
¼   *cup Kahlua (coffee liqueur)*
7   *eggs (4 whole, 3 divided)*
1   *cup sifted confectioners sugar*
1   *teaspoon vanilla or rum*
1   *cup whipping cream or Rich Whip® , whipped*

Sprinkle gelatin over orange juice to soften it.

In a heavy pan, over a low heat, melt the chocolate in the coffee (and the Kahlua if using).

Add softened gelatin and mix until thoroughly dissolved. Set aside.

In a bowl, beat the 4 eggs and 3 egg yolks (saving the whites of the 3 eggs) until light and fluffy — about 10 minutes.

Add the sugar and the vanilla or rum and continue beating for a few more minutes.

Add the chocolate mixture and beat until well blended.

Beat the whip cream until stiff. Beat the egg whites until stiff.

Fold the egg whites gently into the chocolate mixture, and then fold the whipped cream in gently.

Place in a 2 or 2½ quart souffle dish or individual cups, and refrigerate overnight.

Serves 8.

The Ultimate Chocolate Cake

4   bars (4 ounces each) German Sweet Cooking
    Chocolate
½   cup unsalted butter, softened
4   eggs, separated
4   teaspoons sugar
4   teaspoons flour (or matzo meal, or flour for
    Passover)

Preheat the oven to 425° F. Grease a 9x5x3-inch loaf pan, and line with waxed paper.

In the top part of a double boiler, melt the chocolate over hot-not boiling-water, stirring occasionally.

Remove from the heat, and beat in the butter; let cool.

In a medium bowl, with an electric mixer at high speed, beat the egg whites until stiff peaks form; set aside.

In a large bowl, with an electric mixer at high speed, beat the egg yolks until thick and lemon colored.

Gradually add the sugar, beating constantly; add the flour, beating just until blended.

Stir in the cooled chocolate mixture.

With a rubber scraper, gently fold in the beaten egg whites until thoroughly incorporated.

Turn the mixture into the prepared pan. Reduce the oven temperature to 350° F. Bake the cake for 25 minutes.

Let the cake cool completely in its pan on a wire rack. The cake will "collapse," so don't panic. Refrigerate the cake in its pan for several hours.

To serve, loosen the cake by running a spatula around the edge of the pan. Invert the cake onto a serving platter, and carefully peel off the waxed paper. Cut into ½-inch slices.

Serves 12 to 16.

Index

New Recipes

New Recipes

New Recipes

New Recipes